HONEY BEE

D1322280

LIFE CYCLES

Words in **bold** can be found in the glossary on page 24.

THE SECRET BOOK COMPANY

©2018

Written by:
Grace Jones

Edited by:
Charlie Ogden

Designed by:
Matt Rumbelow

HONEY BEE

WHAT IS A LIFE CYCLE?

All animals and humans go through different stages of their life as they grow and change. This is called a life cycle.

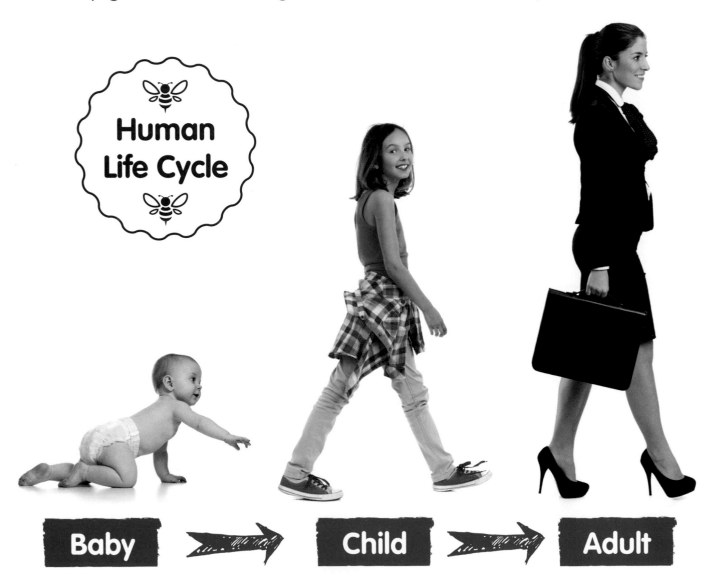

Human Life Cycle

Baby ➤ Child ➤ Adult

WHAT IS A BEE?

A bee is an **insect**. It has four wings which it uses to fly, five eyes and six legs.

Eyes

Wings

Legs

EGGS

The **queen bee** lays her eggs on a ball of **pollen** inside her home. A bee's home is called a hive.

There is only ever one queen bee in each hive.

The queen bee lays one to three eggs in any one cell of the hive. She can lay up to 2,000 eggs a day.

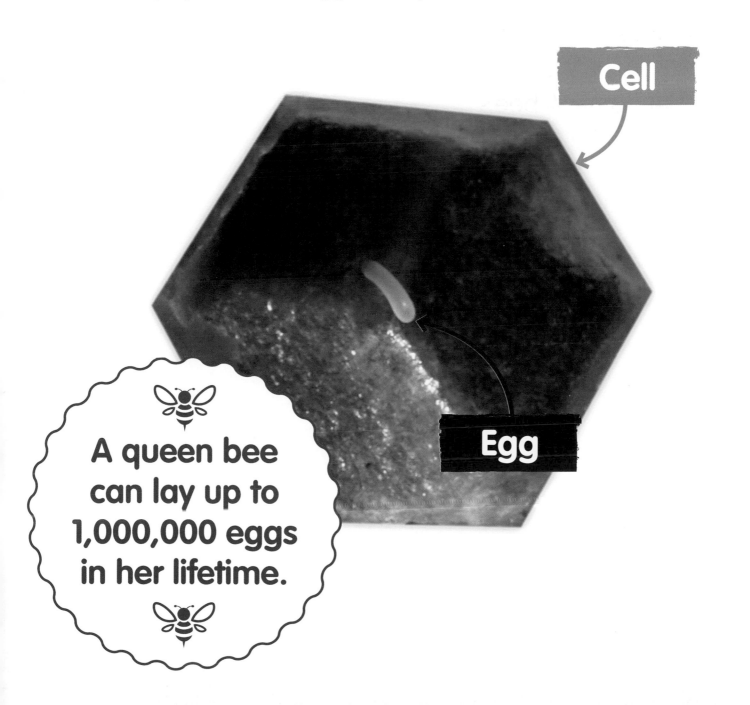

Cell

Egg

A queen bee can lay up to 1,000,000 eggs in her lifetime.

GRUBS

After around three to four days the eggs **hatch** into small, white grubs called larvae. At this stage they have no legs, eyes or wings.

Larvae

Worker bees feed the larvae with **royal jelly** that they themselves produce. After this, the larvae are fed a mixture of honey and pollen known as bee bread.

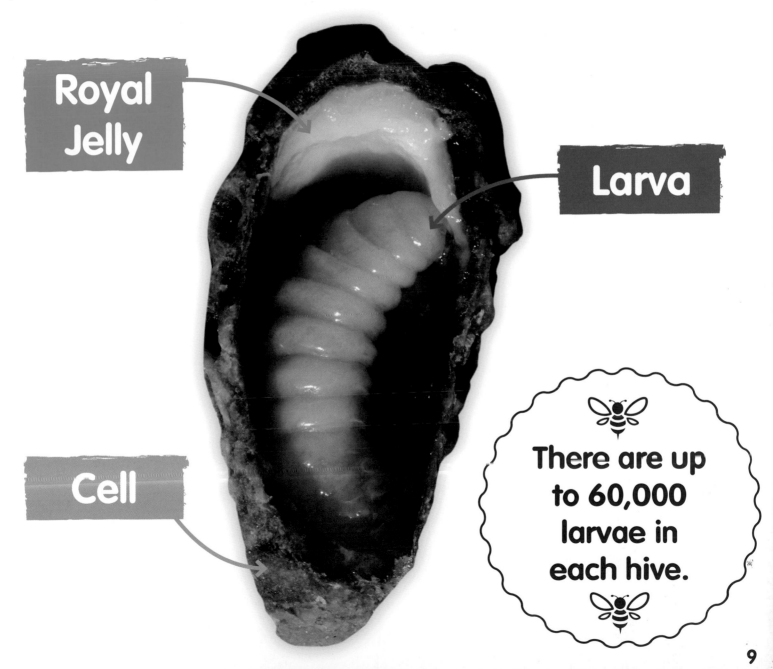

Royal Jelly

Larva

Cell

There are up to 60,000 larvae in each hive.

GROWING GRUBS

The larvae grow very quickly, which means that their skin gets too small for their bodies. They **shed** their old skin and grow a new, bigger skin underneath.

The worker bees feed the hungry grubs.

Worker Bees

After around five days, the larvae have grown over 1,500 times their original size and have shed their skin five times.

CHANGING GRUBS

Once the grub has grown big enough it spins a coat of silk around itself. This is called a cocoon. Workers bees then cover the cell with a wax capping so that they are completely sealed inside.

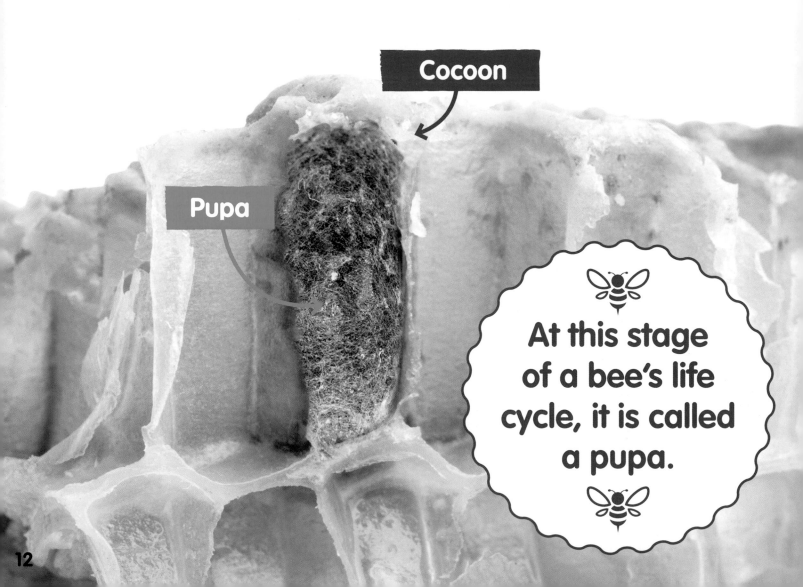

Cocoon

Pupa

At this stage of a bee's life cycle, it is called a pupa.

Inside the cocoon the pupa is changing. Its eyes, legs and wings begin to form and the hairs that cover its body develop.

Inside the cocoon the grub is changing into an adult honey bee.

BEES

After around 12 days, it chews its way through the wax capping as an adult bee. It joins the rest of the hive to begin adult life.

It takes around 15-24 days for a honey bee to develop from an egg into a fully grown adult. It is thought that around 111,000 visits are made to one single bee before it wraps itself inside its cocoon.

Adult Honey Bee

BRILLIANT BEES

Honey bees make the sweet honey that we can eat and buy in shops. Honey is made from the nectar the worker bees collect from flowers.

Honey

There are over 25,000 different types of bee in the world.

In the hive, bees communicate with each other by doing a special sort of dance called the waggle dance. They do this to tell each other important information such as where they can find food outside of the hive.

LOOKING FOR FOOD

Worker bees collect nectar and pollen for their food and bring it back to the hive for the other bees to eat. Nectar and pollen is found in flower heads.

Worker bees carry pollen in special baskets on their legs.

Pollen Basket

Worker bees look for brightly coloured flowers to find nectar and pollen. They drink it using their long tongues, which they use just like a straw!

WORLD RECORD BREAKERS

The World's Largest Bee Hive:

Found In Texas, USA

Size: Over 6 metres Long

6m

Fun Fact: The biggest bee hive ever found had over 500,000 bees in it.

The World's Largest Bee:

Female Leafcutter Bee

Size: 3.8 centimetres

Fun Fact: The Leafcutter Bee is found in Indonesia and they build their hives in termite nests.

LIFE CYCLE OF A HONEY BEE

1 A queen bee lays eggs in a hive.

2 A grub hatches from an egg.

LIFE CYCLES

4 The grub has changed into an adult bee.

3 The grub wraps itself in a cocoon inside its cell.

GET EXPLORING!

See if you can spot any bees in your garden or local park.

The best time to look for bees is in the summer when it is warm and sunny. Watch what they are doing. Are they collecting food?

GLOSSARY

hatch when a young animal breaks out of its egg

insect a small animal that has six legs and four wings

pollen a yellow powder that is found in flower heads

queen bee a bee who is in charge of the hive and is the only one who lays eggs

royal jelly food made by worker bees and fed to larvae

shed when an insect's old skin falls off

worker bees bees that collect food, feed larvae and look after the hive

INDEX